Do Death

For a life better lived

Amanda Blainey

To Gordon Marshall,
the gentlest of men,
with the biggest heart

Published by
The Do Book Company 2019
Works in Progress Publishing Ltd
thedobook.co

Text © Amanda Blainey 2019
Photography © Sue Parkhill 2019
Author photograph © Nicola
Bensley 2019

The right of Amanda Blainey to be
identified as author of this work has
been asserted by her in accordance
with the Copyright, Designs and
Patents Act 1988

To find out more about our company,
books and authors, please visit
thedobook.co or follow us **@dobookco**

5% of our proceeds from the sale of
this book is given to The Do Lectures
to help it achieve its aim of making
positive change: **thedolectures.com**

Cover designed by James Victore
Book designed and set by Ratiotype

Printed and bound by OZGraf Print
on Munken, an FSC-certified paper

A CIP catalogue record for this book
is available from the British Library

ISBN 978-1-907974-67-0

10 9 8 7 6 5 4 3 2 1

Contents

Prologue

I grew up in a household where my parents, who were Sri Lankan, often talked about death and dying. As a child, I did not fear death but was fascinated by what it meant. We had little money so for a cheap day out my mum would sometimes take us to the local cemetery. My sister and I would run about and read the dates and epitaphs on the gravestones; we were curious about what the families had written about their loved ones. We were enthralled by the different shapes and sizes of the tombstones; how some contained entire families who had died a few hundred years ago. Some newer graves had pictures of the person that had died and we often imagined what their life would have been like. The cemetery was not a scary place for us. It was somewhere we could delve into the lives of people who had once lived — and of those who had loved them.

Now, as an adult volunteering in a hospice, it's not so much the death that affects me when I go home at the end of the day, but the life stories of the people I have spent time with and come to know: their complexities, practicalities, joys, regrets, wishes ... and the love. All that comes with life — personified by the friends and family that surround them at the moment of death — is palpable.

Introduction

Somewhere inside all of us is
the power to change the world.

—

Roald Dahl

**Death has a 100 per cent success rate. We can't escape its
inevitability nor can we deny its existence. Yet if we are
willing to have a relationship with and an acceptance of
death it can make us realise how precious life is. When
we have lived a good, meaningful life, it can help us to
let go at the end.**

We have forgotten how to 'do death'. The community
support once provided is no longer there, we distrust our
own instincts and have little guidance to tell us what to do.
We have become swept along by the promise of technology
and medical treatment and no longer regard dying as a
natural process. Death has become institutionalised —
families and community support are on the periphery of
end-of-life care.

Other cultures such as Ireland, India, Indonesia and
Mexico have a very different way of dealing with death and
dying, such as honouring rituals, looking after the body
and finding ways in which to remember their loved ones.
Death is normalised and seen as a natural end to life.
These communities support each other rather than simply
relying on the medical and healthcare professionals to tell
them what to do. Sadly, we've lost many of these rituals,

and our confidence in caring for the dying. We undervalue grieving as an essential component in dealing with death. It's up to us to start doing small things to ignite change and to bring back these forgotten customs.

Having conversations earlier about death means we can be more prepared for when it happens. I started my organisation 'Doing Death' to encourage a dialogue around the subject, even though my actual experience of death itself had been minimal. When I started to volunteer in a hospice, honestly, I was fearful of what I might experience. Once I overcame this fear I found it to be one of the most rewarding and eye-opening experiences of my life. These are some of the biggest lessons I have learned: not to take any day for granted; to take care of yourself and others and not lose sight of what's important; and that we are all connected through life, love and the universal experience of death. Our relationships unite us, give our lives meaning and inspire us.

Death can be our greatest teacher. If more of us were open to the experience of death we would have a better understanding of what it means to die and, in turn, how to live. If we can be better prepared for death, its impact on ourselves and our loved ones can be lessened. And finally, we can *wake up* to our life and begin to embrace it more fully.

This book is a manual for *living*. It is a gentle reminder to start thinking about what matters in death — and in life.

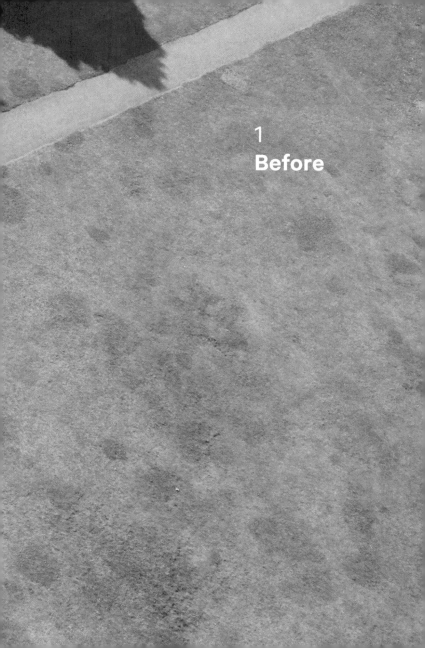

1
Before

> Everyone knows they're going to die but nobody believes it ... so we kid ourselves about death. But there is a better approach: to know you're going to die and be prepared for it at any time. Do what the Buddhists do — ask, 'Is today the day? Am I ready? Am I doing all I need to do? Am I being the person I want to be?'
>
> Mitch Albom

We prepare for milestones like childbirth and marriage, but not death. For instance, have you ever thought about the type of funeral you might want? Or how you would like to be cared for when you are dying?

When broaching a subject as broad and complex as death, a natural starting point is some of these more practical matters. Not only does it make sense to think about them now, rather than when you are approaching death, but it can help with the acknowledgement that death is real and could come at any time. Planning can also help to avoid family tension, fall-outs and anyone having to make difficult decisions on your behalf. And it encourages you to start contemplating what matters to you in your life and your legacy. In this book, my aim is to help you to start thinking about death — your own and those close to you — to become better prepared for it, to know what to expect, and to live more consciously.

Fear

I saw a study that said speaking in front of a crowd is considered the number one fear of the average person; number two was death! This means to the average person if you have to be at a funeral you would rather be in the casket than doing the eulogy.

—

Jerry Seinfeld

Most people aren't scared to die but are scared of *how* they die. Fear is a natural part of our make-up but you can't avoid it — and nor should you. This natural response is needed for protection from external dangers. But fear can manifest itself in your thoughts and distort your view of the world. Confronting those fears head-on can help prevent them hindering your life and holding you back.

The idea that life is impermanent is in itself a scary thought. It can stop us from challenging our feelings about death. If you're one of the many people who fear death, it's worth asking yourself why you might feel that way. Is it based on experiences in the past? Or of someone close to you dying? Could it be based on a fear you have in life? One man who came to a discussion group that I held about death was petrified of it. It was constantly on his mind and getting in the way of him living a normal life. He had never spoken his fears out loud before, but once he did he felt a great sense of relief. Talking about something has the power to release inner conflict and bring about change. Starting to have those conversations and confronting your fears about death may help to dissolve the intensity of it and any preconceived ideas you may have formed.

So often our imagination is worse than the reality. Many of us don't want to acknowledge death because that means accepting that our life is finite. But maybe it's not that we are scared of death but scared of life. If we believe death is when we 'rest in peace' then maybe it's time to embrace our fears, stop procrastinating and enjoy our wonderful, turbulent, complicated life. As the saying goes, we'll have plenty of time to rest at the end.

Acceptance

> No one wants to die. Even people who want to go to heaven don't want to die to get there, and yet death is the destination we all share. No one has ever escaped it. And that is as it should be, because death is very likely the single best invention of life. It is life's change agent. It clears out the old to make way for the new.
>
> —
>
> Steve Jobs

Some people who have been given the news that they don't have long to live — whether it's a couple of years, months or even weeks — may, after the initial shock, start this process by asking themselves, 'What can I do to live well, now that I don't have much time left?' Some overhaul their lives and prioritise their own needs, possibly for the first time, taking trips to places they have always wanted to go and doing things they've always wanted to do. Spending quality time with friends and family, renewing marriage vows, working with charities, even running marathons. It's as if they have a new lease of life. They feel less inhibited and this can be a time of great liberation.

Many of us have never accepted or prepared for death and have existed in a pocket of denial right up to the end of life. Preparing for death starts with acceptance. You may not like the fact that you're going to die but embracing its inevitability is the first step to removing some of the fear and mystery surrounding the subject.

Expectations

Let's start by thinking about our expectations. For example, what does it mean to have a 'good death'? Is a good death even possible? It sounds like an oxymoron. Death is rarely something we want, so how can it ever be 'good'?

A good death might reflect your values and what mattered to you in life. Experiencing a fulfilling life, creating one with meaning, might help you release your attachment to the physical world, your body and your relationships when dying. It might mean being pain-free or surrounded by friends and family. To feel supported, listened to and in comfort. And we're going to look at some of these more closely in the chapters that follow.

Perhaps our desire to have a 'good' death relates to our modern need to compartmentalise many areas of our lives, and to achieve a positive outcome. But death, like life, can rarely be packaged up neatly. Death and dying can be messy, unpredictable, uncomfortable, sudden or drawn out, but by thinking about it now, it's possible to face it with a little less trepidation, whether it's your own or that of someone you love. My aim in writing this book is to help you with some of that.

Preparation and Planning

As I mentioned at the start of this chapter, preparation is a good place to start. It's hard for family and friends to deal with all the decisions that need to be made when someone is dying. Paying for care or immediate needs may require access to banking information. Making informed decisions about medical procedures or treatments can cause huge internal and external struggles, especially if the person concerned is unable to speak for themselves. And without clear instructions, doctors will have to make decisions on behalf of their patient. Without access to relevant information or not knowing the wishes of the dying person, a difficult situation can become even more challenging.

In a sense, thinking about death is about being kinder to your future self and your family. I have seen patients trying to sort out financial, social and legal paperwork from their deathbed, either on the phone or giving written instructions to family members or friends. This is stressful and complicated, especially for transactions that need a signature or physical proof of identity. Waiting until this point to sort out each thing is a tiring, sobering and emotional process. Consider putting things in place while you are living so that people know what you want, and can access important information about you both before and after your death. This is so much better for you and all concerned.

There are lots of factors to consider when preparing for your death. Some are more practical than others and can be done well in advance. Here is a quick overview of some things to think about; you'll find more detail in the Resources section at the back of the book:

- Making a will
- Funeral planning
- Household matters
- Useful information for family and friends
- Decluttering
- Advance care planning
- Business affairs
- Organ donation
- Digital legacy, assets and devices

Let's look more closely at a few of these issues:

Making a will

Before he died, David Bowie organised every single detail of his financial estate and personal wishes. By contrast, the musician Prince hadn't made a financial will. This lack of foresight resulted in his estate bearing the cost of enormous legal bills. Of course, Prince died unexpectedly but, given his wealth, it's surprising that nothing appeared to be in place in the event of his death. In the UK, the government states in bold letters on its 'Making A Will' page: 'If you die without a will, the law says who gets what'. If you have property or belongings that are of financial and sentimental value, or you have children, then it's important to make a will. Unmarried partners do not automatically inherit assets, and married partners with children are not necessarily entitled to the whole estate, so any specific wishes would need to be detailed in a will.

We have all heard stories of the squabbling, fall-outs and ill feeling that can happen when wills aren't made, or are made without family members knowing the details in advance. Money can be loaded with a huge amount of emotional baggage so it's both practical and kind to make a will and discuss its contents with your beneficiaries while you are alive and well.

If you have particular items that you want to go somewhere or to someone, you can specify this in your will. Deciding on who gets what can be a wonderful validation to show what a person meant to you in life.

So when it comes to making a will, be a bit more Bowie, and a little less Prince.

Funeral planning

I know I keep talking about Bowie but he's a modern example of how to prepare for death well. He chose a direct cremation, where his body was collected and cremated with no one present. His ashes were returned to his family who then had a chance to grieve privately and to think about his life and legacy in their own way. There was no ceremony, no funeral and no fuss. By going against the norm in death, Bowie demonstrated his uniqueness in life. A true reflection of someone doing death in their own way.

It's worth bearing in mind that a funeral isn't for you, it's for those you leave behind, so have conversations about it and get everyone on board. They don't have to be lengthy or intense. If you already have a will, keep a copy of your funeral wishes with it. Pre-planning your funeral means your family or friends don't have to make those decisions while they are in the midst of their own grief.

If you are nearing the end of life (due to a terminal illness or very old age) and are feeling creative, you might consider a 'living funeral'. This is a gathering, much like a wake, but one in which you are present. It can be an uplifting way to tell people what they have meant to you (and vice versa) and for close family and friends to start the grieving process. We'll revisit the idea of funerals in the 'After' chapter of this book, and look in more detail at what you need to consider when organising one.

Useful information for family and friends

It's helpful for people to know where to access personal information in the event of your death. Insurance policies or details of household utilities are things we never know about others — why would we? — but it becomes necessary information in the event of someone's death. One option is to create an electronic 'Death' folder on your computer with this information or create a physical folder. One lovely 73-year-old lady I met has created a 'Death Box' which she keeps in her house. It contains all the relevant information her family will need when she dies (you'll find suggested contents in the Resources section at the back of the book). Being organised and ensuring people know where to find this information can make a huge difference.

Household matters

In your home, are you the person in charge of the financial tasks such as bills, internet banking, TV subscriptions etc.? If you're not, how would you cope if the person responsible died? My husband and I are now in the process of making a financial fact sheet with all the information we would both need (i.e. any individual bank account details, investments, warranties, car insurance etc.). We have a financial 'date' every few months (who said romance was dead?!) to go through any additions, changes, budgeting or other financial thoughts for the future. Some people are weird about discussing money but it's important to go through this information with someone you trust. And make sure they know where it's kept for when it's needed.

Business affairs

If you own a business or have business interests that provide you with an income then it's important to look into what could happen to your business and assets if you died unexpectedly. What measures or insurance could be put in place beforehand to protect your family, staff, business partners, and so on? Speak to your accountant, financial advisor or a lawyer to find out your best options.

Decluttering

If you have ever cleared out someone's house after they have died then you will know how much work is involved. It recently took my friend and her family four months to clean out her auntie's house. Going through what someone owned and deciding what to do with all the clothes, books, furniture, trinkets, china, jewellery, garage tools, etc., can be a massively time-consuming task.

If you have any specific items that are valuable or sentimental, you could make a record of who gets what so you can ensure they go to the right person — or you could start gifting them to people now! If you are not ready to do this, think about what will be of value to you or your family in the future and what you should hang on to. Anything else, recycle, sell or give to charity.

Decluttering is a cleansing ritual for your space and mind while you are living. If you can get into the habit of doing it regularly you'll be far more inclined to think about exactly what you are buying, why you are buying it, what you need, and what you already have.

Creating Legacies

Please think about your legacy,
because you're writing it every day.

—

Gary Vaynerchuck

Moving on from some of the more practical matters, have you ever considered how you might want to be remembered? Or about creating something for people to have that reminds them of you when you're no longer here? It might be something to help those close to you now, or future generations, to remember you, your life story and what was important to you. What would you want your loved ones to know about your life? Could you offer them some guidance based on your own experiences?

You can be as creative as you like. Ideas range from a blog post illustrated with personal photographs, or a journal filled with thoughts, quotes and inspirations. You might want to create a memory book or box with sentimental images or items. Or what about a series of voice or video recordings about what you are grateful for, your achievements or particular memories you've shared with family and friends? Perhaps there is something you want to say to them but have never said it in person.

I'm involved in a charity project called 'The Hospice Biographers' that records a dying person's life story chronologically from childhood to the present day. A copy of the recording is given to their family. It's a liberating process. Knowing they are leaving their story behind can help the person let go at the end of their life more fully. This information is often lost over time or misinterpreted through hearsay, so for those that are given the recording, it's wonderful for them to listen to that person's voice with all its nuances whenever they want and for it to become part of the family genealogy.

You may not be making a final album like Bowie's *Blackstar* at the end of your life, but think about what might suit you and your personality. Being mindful of what you might want to leave others when you are no longer here offers you a chance to pause and reflect on where you are in your life now, and things you still might want to achieve.

We're not all Bill Gates, but you might be running a business or working on an idea that could be life-changing for people. These legacies with widespread impact can inspire others and leave a positive imprint or memory of your time here.

So do think about leaving a legacy that your family or generations to come can look at, listen to or read. Families don't share stories in the way they used to, so leaving something for loved ones to remember you by is a powerful act of creation and remembrance. But more importantly, I think we should create legacies in the hearts of the ones we love *while we are living.* Telling our family and friends what they mean to us, how much we love them and being honest about who we are, warts-and-all, can be as much of a legacy as something physical.

There are so many things that really count that don't cost anything: showing people you love them through your interactions, being supportive and sharing your lives together. Simple things such as making people laugh, listening to music together, dancing or holding hands and, mostly, giving people your time. This is how we live on, through the memories we create and the lives that we've touched.

Finding Meaning

Death is there to remind us
of how important each day is.

David Hieatt

In my Doing Death podcast series, Do Lectures co-founder
David Hieatt uses the analogy of a laptop running out of
battery power prompting us to work faster and make
more efficient use of our time. Similarly, death reminds us
how brief life is and prompts us to live more consciously.
In other words, death gives our lives more meaning.

Creating the space to start thinking about the
inevitability of death isn't being morbid; it's a chance to
reconcile yourself with the inevitable and to approach it
without fear or regret. On a more practical level, planning
can make you feel satisfied that you won't be leaving
anyone to second-guess what you want, or with a pile of
stuff to sort out after you're gone. Your loved ones may
thank you for that.

Preparing for death can be liberating. It can help you
to evaluate where you are in life, what matters to you and
how best to facilitate the way you want to live from this
point onwards. Sometimes if a person has had a reprieve
from death or is living with a long-term prognosis you
might see a transformation in how they live — with greater
freedom, authenticity and gratitude.

Have a look at the Resources section in the back of
this book to help you start planning and preparing what
you need.

2
During

There is no such thing as a dying person,
there are living people and there are dead people,
and as long as somebody is alive, as long as they
have any sentience or any sense about them,
you have to expect and allow them to be who they
have always been ... and who they always were.

Elizabeth Gilbert

The next two chapters are ones you can dip in and out of. They provide some practical and emotional advice on what you need to be aware of when you or someone close to you is dying, or to just take in and ponder. Being better informed about this time will help you make decisions about any medical treatment and healthcare, where you want to die and the environmental, physical, emotional and spiritual welfare for yourself or someone you care about when the time comes.

Grief Before Death

When you think of grief do you automatically think of death? We all have pockets of grief in our lives. For instance, leaving school, going to university, the break-up of a relationship, moving house, a child leaving home, or the end of a job or career — they serve as reminders that life is transient. For whatever reason, you can't go back to the way things were, and the change you have to deal with is unsettling and unnerving. But change can provide a shake-up, a challenge, an opportunity or a different mindset.

> If you can learn to accept and even welcome the endings in your life, you may find that feeling of emptiness that initially felt uncomfortable turns into a sense of inner spaciousness that is deeply peaceful. By learning to die daily in this way, you open yourself to life.
>
> —
>
> Eckhart Tolle

Endings allow you to contemplate what happens next. You may find yourself taking stock of where you are and what you want, adjusting circumstances in your life to evolve and move forward on a different footing. Grief in your day-to-day life can offer you the opportunity for self-growth and transformation, as well as an understanding that life and everything in it is impermanent.

When you are dying there is a grieving process for the healthy life you had, the future you imagined and the thought of leaving those you love. Death is the final process of letting go of everything and everyone you have known and will know.

Vulnerability

One anxiety that people have about dying is not being in control of what happens to them. They feel powerless.

Anybody who has given birth or been present for a birth will have experienced the physical, mental and emotional vulnerability that an expectant mother feels. When I gave birth to my three children, I felt an immense humbleness and fragility. The reserve needed from me was something that I had never experienced before, nor knew I was capable of. This was human nature at its most primal and, boy, did I roar!

When people are dying they experience similar feelings. Their body and mind are fragile and yet they have to dig deep for the reserve, strength and bravery needed to transition through this process.

People have been giving birth and dying for as long as humans have existed — our bodies know what to do. When dying we have to deal with physical changes and emotionally make sense of what is happening. Having the best available care to let this process unfold is crucial.

Medical and Natural Death

Dying is not a medical experience, it's a natural one. Sometimes in the world of medicine, death is considered a failure rather than the natural ending to a life cycle.

Medical treatment can sometimes prolong the process of dying in the terminally ill or the very old. It can be invasive, painful, traumatic and unnecessary (for instance, being kept on a life-support machine or needing CPR). Perhaps we should ask what is important during this time: life at any cost or quality of life?

—

Atul Gawande, *Being Mortal*

When it comes to medical treatment and care in the final stages of our lives, we have the power to state what we want. However, there will be a lot of things you won't have foreseen. With advance care planning you can make sure your wishes — or your loved one's wishes — are noted and written down in the medical notes either in the hospital, hospice, care home or at home. And make certain there is an original (with copies) at hand of any advance care planning documents made. This is essential if you or someone you care for has lost the capacity to communicate any preferences for treatment. If the prognosis is terminal then see if a palliative care team is available to offer help and advice. When dealing with medical professionals, explore all options. Be a rebel, use your gut instinct, question everything, be politely demanding, and instigate honest conversations with them. This can help you or whoever is affected make informed decisions about continuing medical treatments or procedures while still maintaining a good quality of life.

What is palliative care?

Often thought of as the last option when someone is dying, palliative care is a fantastic resource to support someone who is living with a complicated or terminal illness or is in the last stages of dying. The role of a palliative care team is to help people live as normal and comfortable a life as possible. They are there to ensure a person maintains a good quality of life. They are incredibly experienced in alleviating pain and managing other symptoms, through measures which can be given alongside any ongoing medical treatment and care the patient is having. Wherever someone is being looked after and in whatever circumstances, it should be possible to access a palliative care team.

Physical pain

To be in physical pain is one of the biggest fears people have when they are dying. Physical pain can be all encompassing, sometimes clouding a person's judgement and their ability to function normally. Managing this pain effectively not only helps the patient, but allows a healthcare team to focus on other factors that may be causing distress.

Nobody should suffer in pain, so wherever someone is receiving care, there needs to be a conversation about how pain can be managed and what help is available.

As well as medical treatments, some hospitals and most hospices offer access to complementary treatments or therapies — for instance, meditation and visualisation workshops, reflexology, acupuncture, massage or cranial therapies.

In addition, there are apps that might be useful to download, such as a meditation or breathing app or a visualisation guide. Often it's easier and less tiring to simply listen than to watch something. It's also worth finding out if there are any massage therapists, energy (reiki) healers or anyone else offering complementary therapies who might be willing to come and offer their time and assistance.

To see someone in pain or to be in pain yourself can be soul-destroying. If you find yourself in a situation of advocating someone's care (or your own), be vocal, ask for pain relief, ask whether other treatments are available, and don't think you are being a burden. Push to see what help is on offer through your doctor, the hospital or a palliative care team. Alleviating physical pain is a game-changer.

Where to Die?

Every man's life ends the same way. It is only the details of how he lived and how he died that distinguish one man from another.

—

Ernest Hemingway

Have you thought about where you might want to die? A hundred years ago, it was more common to die at home surrounded by family and friends. Nowadays, most people die in a hospice, hospital or care home. According to the British organisation, Dying Matters, 70 per cent of people would prefer to die at home, but only 18 per cent fulfil that wish. A huge 60 per cent of people die in hospital, 17 per cent in a care home and 4 per cent in a hospice. It's not always possible to be where you want at the time of death, especially given the care you might need, but it's worth exploring options.

In hospital

Hospitals are sometimes criticised for not handling death well. If you, or someone you are caring for, are in a hospital at end-of-life, you might want to think about the following questions:

- Is a private room available?

- Could I manage the symptoms from home?

- Can family or friends sleep in the hospital?

- Is there a palliative care team available?

- What's the plan for pain relief?

- Is it possible to go home for the final days?

- How could care at home be facilitated?

Seek out options for a more positive outcome. Try to have frank conversations with your medical team about anything that you are unsure about or not comfortable with.

At home

Being in a familiar environment surrounded by family and friends can make you or the person you are caring for feel calmer and more comfortable, so it shouldn't be a surprise that so many people would prefer to die at home. How can we better facilitate those wishes?

In *Do Birth*, midwife and author Caroline Flint advocates home birth because the familiar environment can help the woman in labour feel more relaxed. Most births occur at night or in the early hours of the morning, as being in a quiet and dark room can also help the birthing process. In the hospice I notice that some people die during the night or in the early hours of the morning. Perhaps, as with childbirth, in those hours it feels quieter, safer and more private.

Dying at home may not work for everyone for practical reasons. The house may be unsuitable or too small to accommodate the equipment needed, or someone may be physically unstable, live alone or be too old to care for themselves. If you are the primary carer of a person who is dying, this can be a draining and hard time. Like childbirth, it helps to have someone around who knows what they are doing and can offer practical help. Find out if you are eligible for care at home. Your GP or district nurse should offer support, and look into community palliative care nurses and 'hospice at home' services.

It's reassuring to know that there are a growing number of people around the world who are training to be 'death midwives', or death doulas as they are more commonly known. Their role is to help facilitate the needs of the person dying, and their family, so they have a better, more comfortable and more informed experience. It's the kind of help and support that you might have received previously from your community.

DURING

Hospices

> For human beings, life is meaningful because
> it is a story. In stories, endings matter.
> —
> Atul Gawande

Volunteering in a hospice has given me a wonderful insight into how they deal with death. They can be incredible places. Rather than thinking of hospices as places where you go to die, it's better to think of them as somewhere to help you live. The palliative care team treats patients humanely and will discuss what might be needed to make them more comfortable. Hospices can help to explore options for ongoing hospital treatment, medical care and wellbeing needs, even financial and bereavement advice. Hospice care can provide support for several years through any diagnosis.

Pain is not isolated to physical pain and can be related to emotional, psychological or social factors. In the face of death, it might be the sadness of leaving family and friends behind, feeling like a financial burden or losing faith in one's beliefs. Hospices can provide or recommend help to explore these issues.

It's not widely known that most of the patients under hospice care are outpatients. You can go in for daycare support, be visited at home or be admitted as an inpatient for short periods of time to manage pain or symptoms. This can also give the primary carer a much-needed break.

The atmosphere in hospices is usually comforting, peaceful, calm and reassuring. This alone can make an enormous difference in guiding you through this uncharted territory. We definitely need more of them!

Care homes

In the UK, care homes are either funded privately or by local government. This varies in other countries. It's important to check what you can afford and what is available. Care homes will have access to doctors and other medical professionals but they may not specialise in palliative care. It's advisable to look into exactly what can be offered in terms of end-of-life care and support.

What Happens When You Die?

Every death is different, but usually the physical signs are similar. These signs can be important to help the person dying and those around them identify what is happening. Knowing what's coming can give someone time to prepare for things they might want to say or do.

Dying shows itself in stages. The first is the natural withdrawal from life physically, socially and emotionally over a period of time. The second is when the body starts to shut down in the final stages of living. Changes in breathing are a big indicator. It's reassuring to be aware of these indicators and know that these things are part of the normal process.

First stages (final months or weeks)

— Increased physical weakness: frailty, facial features changing to look more drawn, hair thinning, skin paler.

— Nausea, vomiting.

— Asleep for longer, and more exhausted when awake. Sometimes unconscious but then, when awake, not realising they have been. (Note that medication for pain relief might increase sleeping.)

— Bodily functions become irregular, constipation; or needing management, e.g. catheter.

— Loss of appetite: not wanting to eat as much or at all.

— Changes in behaviour and attitude: more childlike, peaceful, resigned, resolved, loving, sad, agitated, reminiscing, talking about the past and relationships.

— May experience deathbed phenomena: seeing visions,

colours, talking to people you can't see, visions of loved ones, vivid dreams, talking of journeys or of going home.

— Needs and requests: wanting to see people they have not seen in a while, to say goodbye to family and friends, to have a party, plan a day out or look at photographs.

Second and final stage (final weeks or days)

— Decrease in circulation, cold hands and feet, change in skin colour.

— Appetite: stops eating or drinking.

— Smell: noticeable change in person's smell.

— Breathing: person may be unconscious for longer periods of time with irregular and noisy breathing, sounding laboured. Usually the person is relaxed and peaceful at this point. Not being able to clear their throat can produce a sound commonly termed 'the death rattle'. Shallow breathing — then one final out-breath.

— Usually the moment of death is peaceful.

This final stage is a place of existence between life and death, awake and asleep, peace and discomfort, love and indifference, regret and forgiveness, and despair and fulfilment. We don't give ourselves enough credit to be able to navigate this human transition but, armed with the right knowledge, we can.

Accepting and Giving Help

In life, it's hard sometimes to accept help from others, but there are times when you'll need to, and vice versa. When we support our friends, family and community, it builds meaningful relationships and experiences. It is a selfless act and a way to engage your heart and deepen your social and emotional experiences with other people.

Help from others gets us through hard times, offers company, hope, smiles, comfort and distraction. In death, this is no different, and our responses are the same. Pride, desire for privacy, stubbornness and denial are all things that might prevent a person from accepting help that is being offered. It can be hard finding yourself in a situation where you need extra help and support.

When you are dying, don't be afraid to ask for help. Get it wherever you can. You'll find those close to you are only too willing to assist; they love you, so why wouldn't they? Allow yourself to be vulnerable. If they want to come and sit with you, let them, but don't be scared to say when you have had enough, feel tired, are too ill or just need privacy. If you find yourself away from home, you might be confused or lonely, so a bit of company can be comforting and reassuring, even if you are asleep! (And if you are the one doing the visiting, then do consider the above.)

I'm often humbled to see how family and friends rally round to offer support, company or practical help. If you know someone in need, be persistent and be specific. You might say, 'Let me know if you need any help with anything,' but that puts the onus on them to ask, which many people are reluctant to do. Make some specific suggestions about what you think they might need or what you are in a position to offer. For instance, offering to cook for any children involved, drop-offs and pick-ups to hospital or help with paperwork. Small things like this can be a big help.

Carers

Taking on the primary role of a carer can be an exhausting one. It's important that you explore carer support options through government, charity organisations or family and friends.

When you look after someone you love who is dying, it can offer a way to start the grieving process. Gradually letting go, seeing that person physically and mentally shrink away, might help you to become more aware and accepting of what is to follow, and not wanting them to be in discomfort any more.

Showing your love and opening your heart in this way can be a beautiful and healing process for both of you. In the role of carer, try to:

— Be tender
— Be intuitive
— Be soothing
— Be tactile
— Be empathetic
— Be authentic
— Be honest
— Be calm

— Be present
— Be compassionate
— Be respectful
— Be loving
— Be prepared
— Be humorous
— Be a listener
— Expect tears

Saying What's Important and Letting Go

> In the end, only three things matter: how much you loved, how gently you lived, and how gracefully you let go of things not meant for you.
>
> —
>
> Buddha

When people are dying, the life they have led is brought to the forefront of their minds — how they lived, the relationships they had and how meaningful they were. Some people are not ready to leave their life or the people they love. They are scared to let go and transition into the mystery of death. Often, they come to an acceptance of death at a later stage when they have had enough of their physical symptoms.

Telling someone what they mean to you, and vice versa, can be powerful at this time. Knowing you have said what's important can lift spirits and help the process of letting go.

Seeing families not being able to express their feelings to one another can be agonising. Some feel that by initiating these conversations, they are accepting death which will be upsetting to all concerned. If you find yourself in this situation, take the lead. Allow the space for these conversations to take place. Be kind and loving. Tell the person dying what they mean to you and how much you love them.

By the same token, if it's important to say these things at the end of life, then surely we should do this when we are in the midst of day-to-day living. Don't wait.

Death Vigil

Have you noticed that when someone is giving birth everyone is waiting anxiously for news of this life-changing event? Well, it's the same when someone is dying. Family and friends come and go over a period of time to visit the person who is dying. They offer practical help or just sit and talk with them — saying their goodbyes and being present. This usually happens before and during the moment a person dies. The vigil becomes more intense when the person has actively started dying. It's an odd time but there's something ritualistic about it, even if people are not aware of it: it's something they do naturally.

It can be beautiful to witness someone wrapped in this blanket of love. However, it can also be a time where resentment, anger or cracks in relationships resurface and become heightened. Generally speaking, it is a taxing time physically and emotionally for everyone. Events such as death, birth and marriage can really amplify emotions.

A person who is dying can do without others bringing their own issues into that space. If the relationship has been a difficult one, it might take those visiting all their strength and compassion to leave such issues outside the door. But it's good if they can.

In death, it's important to think about who you do and don't want to have around: some family members, friends or someone who works in the care team, for example. If you are acting as an advocate for a person dying, then use your intuition and courage to navigate this space on their behalf.

Be prepared to spend time away from your regular life; you might have to place it on hold during this period.

Creating a Sacred Space and Rituals

Other cultures have certain rituals that are performed when death is imminent. Rituals help us to make sense of and mark significant events and to express our emotions. As well as rituals, the space and the atmosphere can help someone relax, let go and feel protected.

In Tibet, they use singing bowls to work with the energy of the person. In some Buddhist traditions, they think about the good things in a person's life and chant or recite prayers to them. They believe it will mark the transition from death to a person's next life. But rituals can be of your own making. It might be reading a poem or excerpts from a favourite novel, or asking visitors to write notes with loving thoughts and memories to be read out during or just after death. It could be lighting candles in the room or using oils.

What matters to you or someone you might be caring for? What do you think you or they would like? It might be a hand or foot massage, listening to a favourite radio station, holding a talisman or crystal. Some US hospitals and hospices have introduced live music such as a harpist or a choir as part of their end-of-life care. Listening to music or singing together is a powerful tool for transcending the mind and body. In life, music has an uplifting and calming effect, and it can be the same when someone is dying. On the other hand, some people might feel that music is invasive and prefer silence, so never assume. There might be sensitivity to light or sound. Sometimes a person might like to hold a soft toy or something from their childhood for comfort. Other rituals could be putting photos around the room of family and friends, even a family pet. It might even be as simple as opening the window to let some air in or to feel closer to nature. Even breathing in time with someone dying can have a calming effect. Consider things that are familiar that might offer a feeling of security and comfort.

By thinking about the immediate environment of the person dying — whether at home, in hospital, a hospice or care home — it's possible to create a space for them which is more calming, feels safe, familiar and even sacred.

Choosing When to Die

People often die when their loved ones leave the room for a coffee, to make a phone call, or pop home. When people are in an unconscious dying state, they seem able to choose their moment to die. If you have been at the vigil of someone who died when you left the room, this notion might offer some comfort.

Doctors have written about patients dying on their birthdays or after Christmas holidays or once significant people have visited to say goodbye. Of course, you might put those things down to coincidence.

As well as 'holding on', the opposite can be the case. Sometimes when I'm talking with someone who is dying they might tell me they are ready to go and then literally, in the space of a week or less, they rapidly deteriorate. It's as if they have made up their mind and are able to accelerate the process.

Sometimes relatives or friends give the dying person 'permission' to die and they do, not long after that. You can't ignore how powerful the mind is and what it is capable of. In the unconscious death state we might be able to consciously release attachment from our physical body. That's a liberating thought.

What Matters in the End

Most people spend their whole lives asleep and then wake up a few days before they're about to die.

Olivia Bareham, Sacred Crossings

Sometimes it takes death or dying to really start thinking about life. To fully appreciate how good life is. A dying person can become more present in a way they weren't before, prioritising what's important, adjusting their outlook, and becoming more aware of their own mortality. It sometimes takes the profoundness of death to lead them to certain realisations about their life. To see the bigger picture and feel connected to something much larger than themselves. The little things they have taken for granted are transcended from the everyday: sharing a moment, a walk or a cuddle.

Faced with death, love and relationships are intensified. Love is what counts, keeps us connected, and love is what remains. It's the most potent emotion I feel and witness when I am experiencing the death of someone. Not the illnesses people have, but who they love, what they love and what matters to them in life.

We are born with love and we should die with love. To experience warmth, tenderness, empathy, comfort, compassion, to be heard and acknowledged. These things can help lessen anxiety and enable us to transcend the experience of death. If we can better navigate death, we can guide and educate future generations to have a more positive experience of death and a deeper understanding of how to live well until then.

3
After

When do people truly die — when
they stop breathing, or when they're
no longer remembered?

—

Grayson Perry

**There can be a lot to do after someone has died — from
all the paperwork to thinking about the organisation
and planning of the funeral, to what happens to the
body afterwards. How do you manoeuvre through the
effects of grief and how can you support yourself and
others when someone has died?**

Some people throw themselves into the practical matters
after death as a way to maintain a sense of control or
as a welcome distraction. Others are more zombie-like,
sleepwalking through this time and barely functioning
because of the pain, shock and disbelief. We have little
knowledge of what to do after someone has died, so it's
useful to know where to start, and what to consider.

———

What to Do When Someone Has Died

Here are some of the important things that need to be done when someone dies.

— Call the **doctor** within a few hours if the death occurred at home.

— Get a **medical certificate of cause of death** (MCCD) from the hospital, hospice or your doctor (if died at home)

— Did the person who has died give permission for or 'opt out' of **organ donation**?

— Collect the **personal belongings** of the deceased.

— **Register the death** with the local authority of where the death occurred (in some parts of the UK you have to do it within five days). You need the MCCD, the full name, address, date of birth, occupation of the person who died, date and place of death and to provide the full name and date of birth of any surviving partner.

— Obtain a **death certificate** from the registrar (get at least 10 copies if you can for proof).

— Obtain a **burial or cremation certificate** from the registrar (in the UK this is known as the 'green' form).

— **Tell people** about the death: relatives, friends, family employer.

— Check for the existence of any **funeral plan** and arrange the funeral.

— **The coroner** may undertake a post-mortem if death was unexpected, unclear, unnatural or violent.

— Tell all **government organisations** about the death
(in the UK there is a system called 'Tell Us Once' which
informs all government bodies, e.g. HMRC, electoral
services, pensions, benefits, passport office, driver
and vehicle licensing agency (DVLA), council and
income tax, etc.)

— Find out if you have to do a **personal tax return** and
estate tax return.

— **Check benefits:** theirs and yours (yours might be
affected). Check for any bereavement benefits that
might be available.

— Establish if a **will** was made. Take legal advice if **no will**
was made, or it has been lost.

— Find out if there is an **appointed executor** of the estate.

— Cancel all **personal utility bills**, memberships,
subscriptions or anything else they were using or
paying for.

— **Alert banks**, mortgage provider, pension providers,
insurance companies, credit card and store-card
providers, student loans, etc.

— Find out about any **outstanding debts**.

— If your **entitlement to stay in the country** depended
on your relationship status to the deceased, check if
this is affected.

— Find **car ownership information**, tax, insurance
documents, etc.

— Manage, delete or memorialise **social media accounts**.

— Find **mobile and TV contracts** and cancel if possible.

Keeping and Seeing the Body

*There is nothing to be feared from a body, Harry,
any more than there is anything to be feared from
the darkness. It is the unknown we fear when we
look upon death and darkness, nothing more.*

J.K. Rowling, *Harry Potter and the Half-Blood Prince*

Once someone has died, you may want to spend some
time with the body. If they died in a hospital, hospice or
care home, tell the staff what you would like to happen
afterwards and they will help to facilitate this. In hospital
the body will be taken to their morgue and can usually
stay there for up to seven days before the funeral director
will need to come and get it. This gives you a little time to
explore options.

If the death happened at home, you can discuss with
the funeral director what is feasible in terms of how long
you can keep the body with you. You might want the body
to remain at home for a couple of days and be returned
again later on, just before the funeral, to allow people to
say their goodbyes. Alternatively, most funeral directors
have a private chapel or viewing room where the body can
be laid out and people can visit.

Funeral companies may suggest embalming to
preserve the body. It's only a requirement if the body is
being repatriated (brought home) from another country.
Embalming uses chemicals derived from formaldehyde
and is an invasive treatment so needs careful consideration.
If it's being requested by the funeral director then you might
want to question why and not be coerced into something
that does not feel right to you. It's possible to keep the body
in cold storage at the funeral home for a couple of weeks

without embalming. If a coroner is involved you will need to communicate to them any beliefs, wishes or cultural needs you or your family may have in terms of treating or caring for the body after death.

If you were not there when the person died, you may not want to see the body and this is down to personal preference. Some say they would prefer to remember what the person looked like while alive; others argue that it's part of the grieving process and acceptance of their death to spend time with the body. Whatever you do has to be right for you, so don't be hard on yourself whatever you decide.

Caring for the body

Some cultures believe that the point after which someone has died is a sacred time to allow the soul to move on after physical life. After death, you might want to sit quietly with that person, brushing their hair or holding their hand. In Cambodia, for example, Buddhist families often keep the body of their loved one at home for three days and perform rituals like washing and caring for it. During this process the immediate family get involved and help. The period just after death can be an odd time, not knowing what you should do. Small rituals like this can help you make sense of what's just happened and to feel you are doing something intimate and special to honour that person.

The washing or dressing of a body can be done by family members at the funeral home — in which case the funeral director should be able to help; or you might prefer they did this themselves. For those who wash their loved one's body, it can be an emotional last act of love. Washing the body can be a cathartic process and this ritual might provide some time to help you to start adjusting to this new reality.

Burials, Cremation, Alternatives

Cremation and burials are the most popular forms of body disposal. Whatever you decide, you might find that the priorities of you and family members are based on choosing something simple or affordable, or natural and sustainable. And the person who has died may have been explicit in their wishes about the type of burial or cremation they wanted, in which case it's simply a question of carrying out those wishes on their behalf to the best of your abilities.

Burials

Currently you can be buried in a cemetery, burial ground or on private land. You can even be buried in your garden if you own the freehold, though I'm not sure that would help the sale of your house in the future! There are a growing number of natural burial sites in the UK and USA and other parts of the world that offer a greener alternative. These can be beautiful plots of land in forests or meadows and other designated areas. Some of these sites don't allow embalmed bodies and request biodegradable coffins or shrouds. The graves usually have trees or flowers to mark them rather than permanent gravestones. They are more in tune with nature and the surrounding environment. You can even be buried at sea, though there are regulations around this so it's worth looking into.

Cremation

Cremation is the most common but not necessarily the greenest way to dispose of a body. Crematoriums are responsible for releasing into the air emissions of mercury from tooth fillings and other toxic chemicals from embalming the body and materials used in the coffin itself (e.g. synthetics). If you decide on this method you can lessen its impact by choosing a more modern crematorium, biodegradable urns or coffins, and give careful consideration to where the ashes are scattered or buried.

The ashes can be put in a box or an urn and buried in a burial ground owned by either a church, council or privately such as green burial grounds. You could keep the ashes in a columbarium, which is a name given for a storage facility that holds cremated remains. There are some beautiful columbaria in the UK, such as the underground barrows in Cambridgeshire that have been created from natural stone. Keep in mind you will need the cremation certificate to bury the ashes or take them abroad. Sometimes people wish to keep the ashes at home until they are ready to let them go elsewhere.

If you want to scatter the ashes check if you need permission to do so. Also consider when scattering ashes that they can affect the pH balance of the soil and have a direct impact on surrounding plants and water nearby.

Alternatives

Globally we are starting to look at more environmentally friendly and sustainable alternatives to burial or cremation. In the US, there is a process called resomation, or water cremation, that uses an alkali-water-based solution to reduce a body to a white ash. In Sweden, over the next few years they are planning to develop a method using liquid nitrogen to freeze dry a body and then make it into a powder. After that it will go into the soil in a box made from cornstarch or potato that dissolves within six to twelve months. Likewise, in the US there's research being carried out into how we could be composted back into the soil and ecosystem. You can donate your body to science or medical research (but if the body is not suitable you will still need to find an alternative method).

Funerals and Celebrating Life

Funerals don't have to be crazily expensive and how much you spend is no reflection of how much you loved someone. The average funeral in the UK according to Sun Life's (annual cost of dying) survey is £4,798. That's a staggering amount, and avoidable with the right research and some careful thought. If you are planning your own or someone else's funeral, the key is to consider what you or they would want. You may want a traditional funeral with a service, or non-traditional with no service at all — it's entirely up to you. Unfortunately, when most of us plan a funeral it's at a time when we are in the midst of grief and despair. It's hard to make the best judgement call at this point.

Funeral companies are starting to recognise and respond to people's need for more choice, less cost and a more personal approach. A number of smaller companies are emerging that cater for this. Shop around for who can offer the most affordable and accommodating option. Local companies are usually cheaper than national ones. Below are some things you might want to consider.

Funeral director: Make sure you feel comfortable with the funeral company you choose and that they are happy to accommodate your needs. They can be involved as much or as little as you want. They may be able to visit you at home for your initial meeting. You can discuss what kind of service you might want, the type of coffin, and the funeral location. Find out if there is a price option for a more 'simple funeral'. Don't feel under pressure to have the funeral they suggest, which may rack up costs with various add-ons. Think about what you really want and need, and what you can do yourself or allocate to someone else to save money.

Order of Service: This is usually a booklet with the details of the funeral service. It can include songs, hymns, poems or images. You can be creative with this, as often people will keep it as a memento. Having photos of the person who died gives them a presence and provides a reminder of their life.

The service: A eulogy is normally delivered as part of the service. You will need to give some thought about who will write and deliver this, and the tone it will take. Formal or informal? A touch of humour can help to lighten the atmosphere and put people at their ease. What about music, a short video or photos of the person who died? If key people are unable to attend, you could find out if the service can be live-streamed or recorded.

Cars: This is a big expense, so it's worth considering using your own transport to and from the funeral. This can also feel more normal than being driven in black chauffeured cars. Technically you don't need a hearse either, you can transport the coffin in anything as long as it fits! Guests could be encouraged to car-share. It's better for the environment, enables guests to support each other and can provide an opportunity to re-connect if they have not seen each other in a while.

Coffins: While it's most common to purchase a coffin from your chosen funeral directors, you are not bound by what's available there and will find many options online. If a more sustainable funeral is important to you, then look at the materials used to make the coffin, as there are biodegradable options. An alternative to wood could be wicker, cardboard (which you can decorate), even a woollen coffin. There's a huge array to choose from. You can even make your own coffin or use a material shroud that can be made out of biodegradable material like bamboo.

Coffin toppers: You can place anything on top of the coffin: a pair of old shoes, a photograph, knitted or paper flowers, a medal or even a glass of beer! Really, it can be anything that feels pertinent.

Flowers: They can be beautiful and uplifting but it might be worth considering if flowers are something you really want and/or if the cost fits into your budget. Did the person that died even like flowers? Could guests donate money to a worthy cause or charity instead? If you do have flowers, try and use a local florist. Another idea is to have flowers or plants in individual pots that people can take home and plant in their own garden. Doing it this way avoids having an excess of flowers, keeps the costs down and can act as a lasting reminder of the person that died.

Music: This is such a powerful source of inspiration for people and can convey a lot about someone. In death, what would remind you of that person? What did they listen to and what reflected their personality? What do you think they would want the song to say about them? This could be a playlist of favourite songs or even a live performance.

A friend of mine wrote a song for his wife and played it on his guitar next to her coffin in the crematorium. It was intimate, heart-wrenching and one of the most incredible displays of love I have seen. Another had a young family friend sing from the back of the church and her voice soared above the congregation. Music can take you to another place and help you feel close to the person who died. It can also bring your emotions to the surface (which is not a bad thing either). Accessing emotions through music can help people express how they are feeling instead of bottling it up. More often than not, the music is what most people remember after a funeral.

Reception: Usually a gathering or memorial is held after the funeral and burial. It's an opportunity for guests to come together and celebrate the life of the person who has died. You may prefer to hold it at a later date — especially if the funeral service was a small, private affair — or not have one at all. Most receptions are held at home, in a pub, a church room or community hall. Perhaps people could help by making and bringing round some simple finger foods. You might want tea, lots of cake or drinks and nibbles in the pub. Usually this is the time when most people relax, share memories and connect. It's a time to remember the person who has died, just not with them being there, which is the hardest part.

Decoration at the reception: Anything that feels right. This could be something simple, like fairy lights or candles. You might want photo albums on the tables, videos or a slideshow of personal photographs projected onto a wall. Try to keep it simple as setting up the tech can be complicated. And ask others to help so you're not trying to do everything.

If you are arranging a funeral, then think of it as a celebration of the person's life, a ritual for marking their death and to help others accept that it's happened. It creates a lasting memory. In making the funeral more personal and relevant, it's an opportunity to shift mindsets away from the type of funeral that is feared or dreaded (not to mention expensive), to a more economical, sustainable, connected and loving experience.

Grief

> It seems to me, that if we love, we grieve, that's the deal. That's the pact. Grief and love are forever intertwined. Grief is the terrible reminder of the depth of our love and, like love, grief is non-negotiable.

Nick Cave

Where there is love there will be grief; the two cannot be separated. It's inevitable that at some point in your life you will grieve for someone you love. Grief is bigger than us, it's powerful, it's universal and it can be all-consuming. You can't run or hide from it and when it hits, it can be utterly destabilising — taking you into new and uncharted territory.

Partly it's our unwillingness to acknowledge death that makes grief so hard to navigate. Like death, grief is not something most of us know how to deal with, so when we experience the death of someone we love we have little idea of how to feel or even begin to start healing.

There are different levels of grief from the more immediate, raw feeling when death has just occurred to later on when you might be able to integrate that pain into your life and find a new normal. Society expects you to 'move on', to 'be okay', 'get better', 'carry on' as the same person you were before. Time can lessen the intensity of your grief but the reality is that you will never 'get over' the death of a loved one. You learn to rediscover life again, differently. There will be the version of you before, and then after, without them.

Others may hardly grieve at all, as they had already prepared themselves or felt that death was a release from the pain or symptoms suffered by the person that died. There is no rulebook to grieving, everyone does it in their own way.

Mourning is the natural process to understand and make sense of what has happened. Allowing time and space for that pain, finding a way to process your feelings and not denying them is key. In a recent discussion group I held, someone described grief as a puddle of water that they dipped in and out of. Some days they were doing okay and then others not so well, struggling to go out or even to get out of bed. You cannot 'manage' grief, just as you cannot 'manage' love. And, like love, your emotions can be just as crazy, unpredictable and can leave you feeling vulnerable. Death leaves you with a hole in your heart that can never be filled — and the more you loved that person, the bigger the hole. However, life can be rebuilt around this hole, especially with the right support around you.

If the death of someone was sudden, unexpected or traumatic, it can lead to a more complex form of grief that we may feel we can never recover from. We may suffer from post-traumatic stress because of the way in which that person died. This kind of grief can be life-altering. When it gets tricky like this then it might be worth speaking to a trained grief counsellor who will be able to offer help, support and advice.

Experiencing the death of someone with whom your relationship was complicated or complex might bring up a multitude of mixed feelings from regret and anger to sadness, even relief. You might be grieving for the relationship you never had. With this in mind, you could try to resolve any issues you might have with those that are living. For various reasons, my sister and I didn't speak for six years. However, over time, we have slowly rebuilt our relationship. It's not been easy, but we know that we both want to matter in each other's lives.

You can still forgive someone or ask for forgiveness even if the other person won't accept the olive branch. This is relevant both in death and in our everyday relationships. Exploring how you feel towards someone, making peace with them and within yourself; doing this in person or virtually where there has been past hurt can be healing. The act of forgiveness, rebuilding and re-establishing a relationship can be powerful stuff.

Connecting in Grief

How can we even begin to navigate the storm that death brings? Human connection is key, being there for each other, listening and showing up long after the funeral. The grief that people feel can be isolating. Usually most people don't know what to say. Offering reliable support and friendship takes some thought and effort. Doing tangible things like running errands shows that you are willing to help. Give someone examples of what you can offer and then do it.

Be available simply to sit quietly with someone who does not feel like talking. You can't fix grief, but being empathetic and acknowledging their pain speaks volumes. Don't walk on the other side of the road. Cross over, say you're sorry, ask them how they are doing 'today', as each day can bring different feelings and will fluctuate daily. If you take a meal around, maybe you can stay and eat it with them. Give a hug to someone who looks like they could do with one. Sometimes people just want to be held in their grief. Not fixed or made happy, just held.

In her incredible book, *Grief Works*, Julia Samuel says that if you write or speak to someone who is grieving, 'Be open and willing to talk about that death, the person and the loss. Don't try to make the loss less. Voice it. Try to find the words for your feelings. If a chasm has been left in your life, say it, if your heart breaks for them, say it.'

One of my close friends has been grieving for the last couple of years after the death of her father. I have tried to make sure that I have been consistent; I am there if she needs a chat, quick cuppa or food. I know I don't always get it right but I'd rather make mistakes trying to help her through her grief than avoid not being there for her at all. It's a learning process. She calls me 'the feeder' because if she is popping over, I'll make sure there is extra food if she fancies it. It's not hard to do small things like this, and it feels good to help.

Some Dos and Don'ts:

Don't say:
— Everything happens for a reason.
— You'll get over it.
— Look at what you have to be grateful for.
— Time is a great healer.
— It was their time to go.
— They are in a better place.
— It will get better.
— You need to move on now.
— They brought this on themselves.
— You need to be strong.
— Don't be sad.
— I know how you feel and what you are going through.
— You could remarry / have another child.
— You should ...
— You will ...

Do say:
— I'm so sorry.
— It sucks.
— How are you doing today?
— I'm not sure what to say but I want you to know I care.
— I am here for you.
— I'm happy just to listen.
— Call me anytime, even if it's first thing in the morning or last thing at night.

Don't:

— Try to 'fix' them.

— Avoid the subject of their loved one's death.

— Add a religious context, e.g. saying, 'It was God's will, etc.'

— Tell them how great your life is.

— Say, 'Let me know if there is anything I can do,' if you don't mean it.

— Be impatient or frustrated when someone is still grieving years later (there's no timeline).

— Expect any gratitude or recognition in return for your help.

— Question their way of grieving.

— Expect them to talk.

— Make assumptions based on appearance. They may look well on the outside, but don't assume they are on the inside too.

Do:

— Ask the person what they need.

— Use the word 'died'.

— 'Ask questions about the person who has died (although for some this maybe too painful), e.g. What do you miss most? Are you able to talk about their death? Do you want to talk about them?

— Check it's okay to visit and not be offended if they are not up to it. Keep offering.

— Bear witness to their pain and acknowledge their grieving.

— Bring a meal round (be aware that they might not want to eat much).

- Give gift vouchers to a favourite restaurant or grocery store (useful anytime).
- Offer support, not just immediately after the death, but also in the months and years after.
- Remember any significant dates like birthdays and anniversaries (wedding, death).
- Offer companionship.
- Offer to sleep over if that helps.
- Be consistent in your help so that you can be relied on now and in the future.
- Offer suggestions of practical help: running errands, with paperwork, laundry, housework, kid pick-ups, shop for groceries, help with funeral arrangements, lifts, etc.
- Create a care rota between family and friends to lessen the burden for yourself and any guilt from the grieving person. Teamwork!
- Write a card, text or email. This could: say that you are thinking of them; specify a memory or something positive about the person who died; speak from the heart; say that even if you didn't know that person well, it's a gift to hear how they touched others' lives (don't expect a reply).
- Take them out (for a walk, cinema, coffee, etc.)
- Use hugs, hand-holding and eye contact.
- Use sensitivity, compassion, kindness, tactfulness and honesty.
- Give them your time.

Helping Yourself

When you are grieving after the death of someone, be
kind and compassionate to yourself. Allow and ask others
to help and support you. Focus on what's important,
what matters to you, and spend time doing those things
to help you heal. Avoid those people who make you feel
uncomfortable for grieving because of their own opinions
about how you 'should' be grieving. Find your thing, tune
in to whatever might work; even if it's just breathing better,
meditation practice or eating regularly, it could help. Keep
a record of how you feel and what helps. Take each day as
it comes, because thinking about the future or the past can
be overwhelming.

It's important to realise that you are not alone and that
most people have, and will, experience death and grief at
some point in their life. Talking about it with others and
sharing your story can be a relief. Mostly what you are
feeling is normal — even though you may not feel normal!
Society has an expectation of how we should grieve
rather than just allowing grief to be seen as an ongoing
and evolving process. Our culture is one in which painful
emotions are seen as problematic, and instead we should
always be striving for happiness. Permitting your grief is

a way to heal yourself and communicate with the person who has died.

The mind and body are not separate, so emotional pain can show up as physical pain like headaches, heart palpitations, chest pain, breathing difficulties, panic attacks and insomnia. It's important to find coping techniques that can help your mind and your body. Exercise has proven to be useful in dealing with the effects of grief; even a walk outside can bring you out of the fog for a little bit. One of my close friends whose brother died at the age of 47 has taken up running as a way to help process her emotions. She finds it has a similar effect to meditation by calming her thoughts, giving her some time for herself, plus she feels the physical benefits from it. She's never run in her life but it's become an integral part of it now and she loves it. Another friend took up outdoor swimming in the freezing ponds of north London. These routines or daily practices help their mental and physical state. Small things like dancing or singing or listening to music can offer some light when you are in the darkness.

For some people who are grieving, it could be just about surviving and getting through. For others, the experience of death prompts them to do something they have often thought of doing but never have. They might start volunteering or create a legacy in memory of the person who has died. Growth or a 'new normal' can evolve out of pain and it's possible to find a way to live alongside grief. By honouring our pain we remember those that have died through the love that remains.

4
A New Way

We realise that perhaps death isn't the negative thing we have been conditioned to think it is. Death brings the beauty of life into sharp relief. Death empowers us to live consciously from the heart. Death brings us together and inspires conversations that help us put fear aside as we support each other.

Ellen Fein, *The Art of Dying*

How can we shift our cultural consciousness so that death is more accepted as life's natural conclusion? Society needs to find a better way to 'do death', to normalise it, build stronger communities and to create safer spaces to die in.

As well as thinking about and preparing for death, there are small things you can do to instigate change. Such changes might cause a ripple effect reaching those around you and encouraging them to think about their own mortality — and what's important to them now. For example, embracing a more holistic way to look after ourselves in life will inevitably help us to use those practices in death. And just by talking more about it, communities are waking up to the benefits of discussing death together and how sharing our thoughts, fears and experiences can have a more positive effect on how we view death, how we live and what's important in the end.

Life after Death

Humans are wired for both connection and grief;
we naturally have the tools to recover from loss
and trauma. ... I thought about how humans
had faced love and loss for centuries and I felt
connected to something much larger than myself
— connected to a universal human experience.
People need to know that they are not alone.

Sheryl Sandberg, *Option B*

How do you continue to have a relationship with someone after they have died? That person is no longer physically present but the love remains, so how can you keep that connection alive? Some people have conversations in their head or out loud with absent loved ones. Others write journals or letters or wear their clothes to retain a feeling of closeness. Author Elizabeth Gilbert wrote on Instagram that she records voice messages on her phone to her partner Rayya who died. The act of recording it makes her feel that it's being received. She says, 'I get to talk to her, cry with her, laugh with her.'

In Mexico they remember their dead by holding an annual festival called the 'Day of the Dead'. Rather than being morbid it's full of colour and vibrancy; it's a celebration of life not death and a way to acknowledge mutual grief. It's a massive event and brings communities together in expressing their grief, past and present.

I have heard and read about those who have seen birds or butterflies in unusual places or out of context after someone has died. Or objects like coins or white feathers. Hearing a favourite song when they might be thinking about the person who died is also common. Frequently it is something obscure that had meaning only to their relationship. Some disregard it as mere coincidence, but others feel it is a sign from their loved one.

My good friend's mum died a few years ago. The day after she died my friend received a text with just an emoji of a smiling face sent from her mum's phone. The phone was no longer in use and her mum had never used emojis so it came as an odd but reassuring surprise! Similarly, when we recorded my podcast, David Hieatt told me about his dad's love of nature and birds, especially robins. His dad died a few years ago but as David does his morning workout he often sees a robin outside the window. It makes him feel like his dad is looking out for him. Seeing or finding something that reminds you of the person that died might make you question your beliefs. Whether you believe in an afterlife or not, these occurrences can evoke a memory of a person that may offer some comfort and help us to hold their memory close.

Today, there are online companies that allow a person who is dying to make recordings to be sent to their family and friends after death, or on important dates such as birthdays or anniversaries. That might seem a bit creepy, but the response has been positive as people search for ways to remember loved ones after death.

In 2011 a tsunami killed 15,000 people, including many in the town of Otsuchi in Japan. One resident, Itaru Sasaki, created a disconnected phone booth in his garden to communicate with his cousin who died in the tragedy: 'Because my thoughts couldn't be relayed over a regular phone line, I wanted them to be carried on the wind.' Since then more than 10,000 visitors have come to use the phone as a way to express their feelings. Studies have shown that suppressing our emotions can affect us physically and emotionally, so finding a way to connect

and remember those who have died can be healing.
We just have to accept that the way in which we connect
to someone after they died will be different than before.

Finding Space to Talk

Death has the potential to offer opportunities
for profound healing and transformation.
Death is clarifying. Being mindful of death
helps us to identify our highest priorities.

—

Jon Underwood

When people get together to talk and share experiences
with each other, amazing things can happen. The feeling
that you are not alone can create a shared sense of
belonging and connectivity. In particular, being able to
talk about death can be a transformative process as it
allows you to explore your fears on the subject and
discuss it openly.

A great example of this is the pop-up event Death
Café, which was set up in 2011 by London resident Jon
Underwood. It was created as a space for people of all ages
and from all walks of life to come together, eat, drink and
talk about death with complete strangers. I run a death café
close to where I live and people often describe the event as
uplifting, 'life affirming', 'thought provoking', 'insightful' or
'funny'. Having an authentic chat about death leaves people
feeling a bit lighter, more positive and as if a weight has been
lifted. Through one man's initiative to create social change,
the death café movement has been a major contributor in
helping people to discuss death around the globe. To date
there are around 7,600 regular death cafés in 64 countries.

Talking about death has a clever way of reminding you of what matters in life and that you still have time left on this planet. That reminder makes you feel awesome! But what can you do to gently start having those conversations with your family and friends, not just in a designated place but wherever you feel comfortable? When I tell people about my organisation 'Doing Death' they usually laugh first at the name and then, wherever we are — in a shop or out for dinner — they are keen to tell me their experiences of death. It's hard for them to stop once they start. It shows that there is a real need and a desire to share our experiences.

Giving yourself permission and space to talk about death is one of the simplest things you can do to initiate change and break down the notion that death is something taboo.

Language

Being mindful about the language you use to describe death is probably not something you have thought about much. When you refer to someone who has died do you use expressions such as 'passed away', 'lost' or 'departed'? Euphemisms like these have become the norm to describe death. Experts in the field (funeral directors, doctors, palliative care specialists) commonly use them when discussing it.

But people who die don't get lost, they die, and it's important we use the words: died, death, dying. People don't use alternative words when someone has given birth so why has it become normal to describe death as something else? The avoidance of using the right terminology to describe death mirrors how we try to hide the subject. Saying 'died' shouldn't be awkward or offensive. It might make death seem more real but that's because it is.

Great communicators from Gandhi to JFK showed how the power of speech can make a difference. It's surprising how using the right words becomes normal when you make a conscious effort to do it.

Educating Children

One in five children will experience the death of someone close to them by the age of 18. That's a high number for us to ignore. Sex education is given in schools and young people learn about birth and what happens naturally to their bodies as they grow older. Knowing about death and how we grieve is another essential tool for life, yet the subject is rarely discussed with children. Identifying the biological signs of death and dying, touching on end-of-life planning and how we grieve would be valuable in the UK's national curriculum in Personal, Social, Health and Economic education (PSHE) classes and their equivalent worldwide.

But we can start the education process at home. I don't constantly talk about death with my children, but they do ask lots of questions: 'What happens when you die?' 'Where do you go?' 'What's a funeral like?' 'Can I go?' How we answer these questions depends on the child, but answering as honestly as possible is valuable for everyone. Obviously it's important to take sensitive characters into account and not scare children, but in our house death is treated as a normal topic of conversation. Think about letting your kids go to a funeral if it's a grandparent or someone they knew and loved. It will help them to process death. Most young people are more resilient than we give them credit for.

My close friend's partner and father of her three boys died unexpectedly a few years ago. It was incredibly hard for her children but after a lot of thought and taking advice from child bereavement groups she decided to involve them in the funeral to help them accept the reality that their father had died. She chose a white biodegradable cardboard coffin and the children spent a couple of days decorating it with drawings and images in brightly coloured pens. The coffin looked beautiful, and it felt much more personal and less austere when it was carried into the service. Her children were okay about decorating the coffin and it seemed to help make the funeral a less daunting experience for them.

Bereavement specialists talk about having a level of honesty with children in dealing with death and how you talk to them when someone they know has died. Often their imagination is scarier than the reality. Be prepared for them to be emotional. Listen, be gentle, and remember to use the correct language to describe death. There are charities and child bereavement groups that are available to offer advice and guidance on the phone, online or in person. It's worth using these valuable resources. In addition, there are some great books that have been written specifically to introduce children to the subject of death and what it is. You'll find more information in the Resources section at the back of the book.

Having an open conversation earlier with children about death can help them accept it as part of life. And if you happen to have any pets that generally don't live very long (like a goldfish), it's a great way for them to learn about life and death.

Doing Death Better

If death has become such a taboo subject in our society then it's no wonder that how or where we die hasn't been given much thought. Hospitals are not designed for it, despite being the place where most people die. More end-of-life training is needed for doctors and nurses to help them better communicate with patients and their families about their prognosis. Healthcare professionals could be more compassionate, empathetic and clearer in their communication about care and treatment. This could lead to less suffering and a better experience of death in hospitals. Governments could increase funding into palliative care strategies and create more hospices and community initiatives to help care for the dying.

Taking a more active role in our community and its welfare can make us think about how to look after each other better. If you know someone who is dying in your community, don't be scared or shy away, go and see if there is anything you can do to help. Some people feel lonely, anxious and afraid, but having someone there (even if it's for an hour) to talk, listen or just sit with them can be comforting.

If this does not appeal, you could get involved in fundraising for your local hospice. Have a look and see if there is anything you can do to volunteer in local hospices, hospitals and your community. You might not think you can make a big difference, but your help is more likely to make an immediate impact rather than waiting for governments to initiate better models for dealing with how people are dying in the modern world.

Holistic Living and Dying

Death needs to be seen more as a natural, human process if we are to improve our experience of it. Living in a more holistic way to feed, replenish and heal our inner being can give us better tools to cope with life, and therefore death whenever it comes. Giving ourselves time for reflection, contemplation and quiet is as important in life as it is around the time of death.

In the 'During' chapter we looked at how complementary therapies, treatments and counselling as part of hospice care offered a way to help deal with physical pain. They are also useful tools to cope with the emotional baggage accumulated in life and the anxiety or fears associated with dying. Such practices include:

— Meditation
— Improved diet
— Breathing techniques
— Energy healing (e.g. reiki)

— Exercise
— Visualisation
— Hypnosis
— Counselling
— Psychotherapy

These practices can be powerful in releasing tension, relieving symptoms or simply putting someone in a better frame of mind. However, patients with access to these therapies are sometimes hesitant to use them, especially if they have not adopted these techniques or resources before in their lives. It can be a bit of a minefield thinking about what might work or where to start, but it is worth looking into.

Some people who work in end-of-life-care (such as death doulas) might suggest using techniques that include using visualisation, meditation and breathing to guide people to a safer place both mentally and physically. When I have sat with someone who is dying, I can see them first physically retreating from their external world and then mentally becoming more internalised. Being able to access a peaceful state of tranquillity can help you cope with pain, anxiety and disconnecting from life when you are ready. And in living, it can help you cope with everyday stress. Don't wait until you are dying to do the work of a lifetime.

5
Conscious
Living

As you get older, the questions
come down to about two or three.
How long? And what do I do with
the time I've got left?

David Bowie

**Buddhists talk about the concept of experiencing each
night as a small death and waking up to a new reality the
next morning. They view the new day as a chance to do
things differently and to let go of anything that doesn't
serve you.**

Conscious living is about waking up to how you live, being
aware of your remaining time and living it passionately,
mindfully and connecting with yourself and others. It
doesn't mean being the most successful or the wealthiest
but rather having a meaningful life doing what matters to
you, and being who you want to be.

Life Review

I hope there are days when your coffee tastes like magic, your playlist makes you dance, strangers make you smile and the night sky touches your soul. I hope there are days when you fall in love with being alive.

Brooke Hampton

Part of accepting death when you are dying is accepting the life you've had in order to let go of it more easily. The big question is, was it a good one?

In his book *Do Disrupt*, author Mark Shayler has an exercise which involves cutting up a paper measuring tape. You start at the number representing your age now, discarding the part of the tape measure that comes before. Then cut the remaining section at the age when you think you might die (based on family history, or there are websites that will forecast this). Seeing what's left in black and white like this can be quite a stark reminder of how much time you have left. It makes you realise how precious that time is and how fast your life goes. Every moment counts.

I met a lovely lady who was in the last few weeks of her life. She was in her mid-sixties. Her husband told me about the plans they'd had to go travelling and to live in the countryside after she retired. She became ill not long after retiring and her health rapidly deteriorated. They never got to accomplish any of their plans. Often people wait until they retire to do something they love. Do it today, not in years to come. Don't procrastinate!

One exercise you could do now is to write your own 'living obituary'. What's your life story to date? Do this chronologically from birth to the present. You can mark significant events — positive and negative, qualities, relationships and other influential people. What would you say about your life so far? It might prompt you to think about some of the following:

— What am I proud of?

— Does my life have meaning and purpose?

— Am I content?

— Am I doing what matters to me?

— Do I spend quality time with and appreciate those I love?

— Am I the person I want to be?

— Do I live a life for myself or what others expect of me?

— What can I learn?

— Am I using my time wisely?

— Do I help others?

— Am I a giver?

You are the maker of your own story. If you want to rewrite it, be conscious of your thoughts. How do they make you feel? If you tell yourself you can't do something then that's what you'll believe. If you want to make changes in your life, to live better, allow yourself to be brave, think about a new reality, then do one small thing every day to create it. What will your remaining story be?

Relationships and Connection

But it might just save your life,
That's the power of love.

Huey Lewis and the News

In the United States in 1938, a study began to look at the lives of 724 men over a period of 75 years. The men came from two different social backgrounds: half were from Harvard College and half were from Boston's poorest, most disadvantaged neighbourhood. The study looked at all aspects of these men's lives, including work, home life and health. The results showed that it wasn't their status or achievements that kept them healthy and happy. It was their relationships and social connections with family, friends and their community. It found that loneliness and isolation shortened life. And it wasn't just the connections that mattered, but the quality of them. For instance, a toxic marriage could result in bad health and unhappiness. The relationships that stand out when someone is dying are those in which a person is surrounded by love, support, comfort and camaraderie. People who have no one are generally the hardest to bear witness to. We thrive on connection with others. It nourishes and opens our hearts.

Who is important in your life? Think about the people you have around you and if they are a positive influence in your life. Then think about your work/life balance (if such a thing exists). If you don't think you are spending enough time with family and friends, can you do more to address this?

When you do spend time with someone, make that time count: put your phone away and fully engage. Social media and the accessibility of technology are supposed to mean we are more 'connected' than ever before to a wide network of people. But how meaningful are those connections without real, tangible, honest interaction?

Relationships are complicated and intricate at times. Yet loneliness is an epidemic: we need each other. Make plans, go and see people, and when you get there talk, listen, be supportive, have fun, be yourself and be loving.

What Gives Our Life Meaning?

'It's the same with life and death,' Death said.
'What would life be worth if there were no death?
Who would enjoy the sun if it never rained?
Who would yearn for day if there were no night?'

Glenn Ringtved, *Cry, Heart, But Never Break*

The pursuit of happiness often ignores that other emotions like sadness, anger, vulnerability or jealousy are integral to the human experience. It's ying and yang, light and dark, you can't have one without the other; even a black hole has light in it. Good and bad experiences give your life meaning and create opportunities for growth and transformation. It's a bit like grief. All you can really do is surrender to and honour that emotional pain and suffering until it passes. Denying negative feelings doesn't make them go away, they just find another way to show up in your life as either physical symptoms or suppression that can manifest in addictive behaviour. In her TED talk 'There's More to Life Than Being Happy' Emily Esfahani Smith asks, 'Can chasing happiness make people unhappy?' She describes happiness as feeling good in a moment whereas having meaning in your life is long-lasting and makes you think about others and being your better self.

Not only can meaning be found in human connection and creating a new story for yourself, you can also find it in having experiences which transcend the everyday. These experiences bring clarity, perspective and inspiration. Things like yoga, meditation, art, music, exercise, singing, or attending a religious or spiritual gathering. Anything that makes you feel like you are connected to something bigger than you can be meaningful. It might spark you to dream, create, imagine or just be. I went on a yoga retreat at a time when I was trying to come up with a name for a new venture. It was at the end of a session during *savasana* (the relaxing bit) that I saw the words 'Doing Death' in my mind embedded within an image of the solar system. I had been trying to think of a name for months! But in that moment of space and transcendence I had utter clarity.

Most people on their deathbed don't say they wished they had worked more. But work is a big part of your life, so make it count. Try and do something you enjoy, get paid for it, and if you don't love it, see if you can change it. Make time to do something to help and inspire others. Find something that matters to you, find your purpose, find contentment.

Authentic Living

Our Western society tends to focus on the new and discard the old. This applies to both the objects we consume and to the people that surround us. Revisiting how society treats the old and how we can live more sustainably can inspire us to live better.

Ageism

We fight the signs of aging with the next best thing in anti-aging products or even plastic surgery to look and feel younger. We hate the idea of looking and getting older. But this is just a symptom of a larger intolerance. The elderly are not embraced and are often ignored, while the younger generations perceive themselves as busy living and doing. Is it because the very old in our community remind us that death is not far away? We push the thought of getting older away from our consciousness and in doing so fail to take better care of our current aging population. Sadly, the elderly often die lonely because many of their friends have died and family have moved away. We are living longer, so this is something that will affect us all.

My mum worked in an array of old people's homes for most of her life. As small children, my sister and I often went into work with Mum and loved bouncing on empty beds and running up and down the long dormitories that the residents slept in. But most of the time we spent chatting with them. It was magical; we were spoiled, played with and felt appreciated. In very old age, life's purpose is not as clearly defined. Our roles shift from husband to widower, mother to grandmother. One compensation for this loss of roles is that people have more time to just 'be' in the present moment.

When I was a teenager I was asked to visit an elderly person in the community as part of a school initiative. It meant that I missed PE lessons that I disliked so I decided to give it a go. I met a neighbour called Violet who was in her eighties and lived on her own. Her family had all moved away and she was fairly isolated. I asked her if I could visit twice a week and she agreed. From these visits, Violet found some relief from her loneliness and in return I found a sanctuary from my turbulent teenage years with someone who listened and offered her wisdom and life experience (good and bad).

The young and the old have a lot to give each other. Think about a positive relationship between a child and their grandparents. In some countries such as Sri Lanka and India the grandparents routinely live with their families until they die. I have fond memories of my grandfather making us sugar sandwiches. But mostly I remember him just being around and helping out with my parents busy schedule. If you don't have access to grandparents, is there a way to get yourself and children out there and more involved with the elderly in your neighbourhood?

Consumerism and sustainability

As well as thinking about how we can dispose of our dead more sustainably, one of the ways we can live better is to think about how our lives affect our planet and, in turn, the people we share it with. Our constant accumulation of 'stuff' begs the question: is this just another denial of our own mortality? All too often there is a desire to acquire more and more without any thought about what happens to it all when we die. Our time here is not permanent but what we leave behind might be.

Our consumer habits and the environmental impact of manufacturing, distribution and waste have created some huge problems. We have been conditioned to think that buying products can provide us with status, meaning, value and stability. There is a massive debt crisis partly brought on by living beyond our means. You can't take anything with you when you die: you come into life with nothing and you depart with nothing. How often do you stop and think about what and how you are consuming? You're not going to be here to see the damage you've caused, but others may already be experiencing it.

Much of what we buy doesn't last long, breaks or ends up in landfill. Buy less of what you don't need or that doesn't serve you any purpose. Not many people will remember that dancing flower you bought them years ago, but they will remember your company and laughing with you. Fewer presents, more presence.

Nobody wished they had made more money, worked harder or bought more things. In short, they were not concerned with what they had consumed. If I learned any one lesson from my conversations, it is that meaning does not come from consumption, but creation. The meaningful life is one that gives more than it takes.

Claudia Bicen

Death as a Teacher

In the Richard Curtis film *About Time*, the men in the family have the ability to time travel to revisit and relive moments in their past. In the final scene, the son (played by actor Domhnall Gleeson) says, 'The truth is I now don't travel back at all, not even for the day. I just try to live every day as if I've deliberately come back to this one day to enjoy it as if it was the full, final day of my extraordinary, ordinary life.' *Groundhog Day* is a film with a similar message. It's about one man reliving the same day every day until finally he realises what matters.

Often, when I step outside the hospice after a shift I have the sensation that I am experiencing things differently. I notice the clouds in the sky, the light reflecting on leaves, the wind on my face. It's a curious feeling. Our day-to-day lives are just as important as what we strive for. I hold my children a little tighter on those days and I feel grateful. An awareness of death has given me an appreciation for the simple things in life.

It's not practical to live each day as if it's your last, but you could try to spend one day with this mindset. How might that make you feel? A day filled with micro-moments that count. Perhaps you'd tell those close to you what they mean to you. You might have more of an acceptance of your own and others' flaws. Or be less bothered by the challenges that the day brings. Maybe you'd be less self-conscious, or be more authentic. It might prompt you to be kinder and more compassionate to those around you.

Death gives life clarity. It allows you to live more in the present and be able to see the everyday beauty in people and experiences. If your head spends too much time in the future or retreating into the past, you forget to live in the present, with your heart.

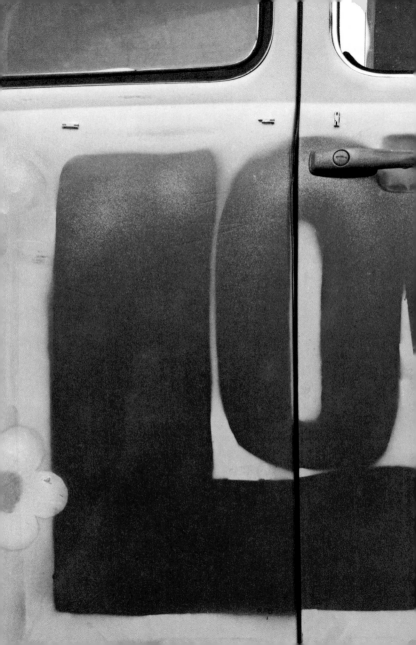

Conclusion

The greatest thing you'll ever learn
Is just to love and be loved in return.

—

Nat King Cole (from 'Nature Boy' by Eden Ahbez)

My hopes are for a future where death is more accepted and, in turn, life is celebrated. We need to 'do' death better. When we are dying, we need others to honour who we are and how we live and have lived, and to understand and accept that we are all individual human beings. By giving compassionate and improved care, and by listening to what the dying need, we can find better ways to support them. In doing so, we leave a more positive legacy of how we die.

When someone dies we are reminded of the finality of life, and not to take anything or anyone for granted. Death is a full stop, a deadline, a chance to know that what you do in life counts. It is a reminder to keep trying to live the life you always wanted to. Denying death is to deny living, as you put things off to another day in the belief that there's always more time.

By reading this book you have already started your conversation with death. I hope it will inspire you and those you care about to put things in place for a better death — and life. Life is challenging and pushes us to our limits, but it's also full of the good stuff like joy, creativity, abundance, inspiration and transcendence. What makes yours a good life? Most importantly, if human connection and love are the fundamental components to a contented and meaningful life, then how can you nourish those relationships?

Simple things like kindness, empathy, authenticity, humbleness, honesty, openness, bravery and vulnerability; they all matter. In cultivating richer connections with your family, friends and wider community you allow yourself to feel greater love for yourself and for others. Death is painful because of how much we love, but love is what counts, in life and at the end.

Resources

Advance Care Planning

You can put things in place verbally, and in writing, to let people know how you would like to be cared for and your medical preferences for treatment in unexpected circumstances caused by injury, illness or from a terminal condition that might leave you unable to express your wishes. It is advisable to write your wishes down and give a copy to the person or people allocated to act on your behalf — partner, parents and so on. Setting up a lasting power of attorney is a way to ensure that your wishes are upheld if advance care planning documents cannot be found or if you are unable to communicate. It can be carried out in a number of ways:

Advance Statement (not legally binding)

An advance statement tells people about your wishes and beliefs, and how and where you would like to be cared for. You can also nominate a person to speak on your behalf. An advance statement can be in the form of a discussion or put in writing so your family, friends and anyone involved in your care are informed. You are advised to add your name, address and date of birth, and to sign it. These wishes should be documented either in your medical notes or somewhere accessible in your house; however healthcare professionals are not legally bound to follow these instructions.

Advance Decision to Refuse Treatment (ADRT. Legally binding)

An advance decision is a more specific legal, written statement expressing your wishes to refuse any future medical treatment. It would come into effect when an individual has lost capacity to give or refuse consent to a treatment. This document should be accessible to yourself, your doctor, healthcare team and anyone who should be contacted in case of emergency. In some areas, health or palliative care professionals are able to electronically record it (sometimes referred to as an Electronic Palliative Care Co-ordination System) in advance so that you have an ADRT in place. You do not need a solicitor to make an ADRT.

Do Not Attempt Cardio-pulmonary Resuscitation (DNACPR)

You can fill out a DNACPR form from your doctor if you do not want to be resuscitated in the event of a cardiac arrest. Without one a healthcare professional will always attempt CPR. You need to have the original document in a visible place and a record of it stored with your doctor, healthcare team and anyone you think should have one. To make this legally binding you would need to include the preference for DNACPR in your Advance Decision to Refuse Treatment form.

Lasting Power of Attorney

This is appointing someone you trust the legal authority to make decisions on your behalf if you no longer have the capacity to do so. There are two types of lasting power of attorney: Health / Welfare and Property / Financial Affairs. You can choose to make an LPA for one type or both.

Digital legacy, assets and devices

We all have a digital footprint. It consists of three parts:

1. **Digital legacy** — which can be social media (Facebook, Instagram, Twitter, LinkedIn etc.), photos, blog or website, email accounts, online banking and other financial accounts.

2. **Digital assets** you may have licensed such as Cloud backup or storage systems like Dropbox and subscriptions such as Netflix or Spotify.

3. **Hardware devices** — phone, tablets, computers, laptops.

You need to consider what you want to happen to your digital legacies, assets and devices, which all have usernames and passwords. How would someone you trust access this information to close accounts and archive data.

Useful information for family and friends

The following items could be placed in an electronic folder or in your 'Death Box':

- Copy of will
- Copy of any advance care planning documents
- Copy of lasting power of attorney
- Birth certificate and any other relevant certificates (marriage, divorce, etc.)
- 'What to do when someone dies' information and links
- How to get probate
- Wills of parents
- Land registration deeds
- Trustee documents
- Information on investments / stocks
- Mortgage details
- Location details of passport, state pension and driver's licence
- Insurance and pension plan policies
- Where to register death (local council)
- Funeral plan plus appointed funeral director (if chosen)
- GP contact details
- Notice for newspaper
- Solicitor contact details
- Accountant contact details
- Bank details / credit cards
- Schools attended
- NHS number
- Location of will (if not in death box) and any advance directive (statement or decision)
- Details of benefits received
- List of relatives or friends to contact
- Details of memberships
- Utilities information
- Subscriptions (inc. online)
- Personal and business tax information
- National insurance number
- Direct debits list
- List of who receives sentimental or valuable items (if not in the will)

Websites

Planning
Tell Us Once via *gov.uk*
compassionindying.org.uk
moneyadviceservice.org.uk
  (deaths)
dyingmatters.org
safebeyond.com
mylivingwill.org
digitallegacyassociation.org
deadsocial.org/resources
gov.uk/power-of-attorney
nhs.uk > conditions > end of
  life care
organdonation.nhs.uk
hta.gov.uk
beforeigosolutions.com
farewell.com
advancelifecare.com (Aus)
goodtogopeace.org (US)

Bereavement
UK

bereavementadvice.org
thegoodgriefproject.co.uk
tcf.org.uk
  (Compassionate Friends UK)
cruse.org.uk
childbereavementuk.org
childhoodbereavement
  network.org.uk
winstonswish.org.uk

Australia
grief.org.au
griefline.org.au

United States
childrengrieve.org
hellogrief.org
modernloss.com

Support
hospiceuk.org
getpalliativecare.org (US)
caringinfo.org (US)
eldercare.acl.gov (US)
carersuk.org
ageuk.org
bhma.org (British Holistic
  Medical Association)
contact-the-elderly.org.uk
eol-doula.uk
lwdwtraining.uk
  (UK death doulas)
soulmidwives.co.uk
  (UK death doulas)
inelda.org (US death doulas)
chaliceofrepose.org (live
  music for the dying — US)
cancerresearchuk.org
mariecurie.org.uk
macmillan.org.uk

Legacy
thehospicebiographers.com

Funerals
naturaldeath.org.uk
funeralzone.co.uk
aboutthefuneral.com
lastminutemusicians.com
compassionatefunerals.co.uk
poppysfunerals.co.uk
localfuneral.co.uk
scattering-ashes.co.uk
goodfuneralguide.co.uk

Alternatives to burial and cremation
irtl.co.uk (cryomation)
resomation.com

Read

Being Mortal
  by Atul Gawande
Big Magic: Creative Living, Beyond Fear
  by Elizabeth Gilbert
Don't Sweat the Small Stuff
  by Richard Carlson
Funerals Your Way
  by Sarah Jones
Grief Works
  by Julia Samuel
It's OK That You're Not OK
  by Megan Devine

The Life-Changing Magic of Tidying
  by Marie Kondo
Natural Death Handbook
  by naturaldeath.org
Smoke Gets in Your Eyes
  by Caitlin Doughty
The Soul Midwives' Handbook
  by Felicity Warner
The Tibetan Book of Living and Dying
  by Sogyal Rinpoche
The Unwinding of the Miracle: A Memoir of Life, Death and Everything That Comes After
  by Julie Yip-Williams
With the End in Mind: Dying, Death and Wisdom in an Age of Denial
  by Kathryn Mannix

For children
Cry, Heart, But Never Break
  by Glenn Ringtved
The Harry Potter Series
  by J.K. Rowling
The Heart and the Bottle
  by Oliver Jeffers

Listen

Podcasts
Griefcast — Ep.14
  Robert Webb
*The Adventures of Memento
  Mori* — 2.1 Worm @ the Core
Goop Podcast — Ep.1
  Oprah Winfrey 'Power
  Perception and Soul Purpose'
The TED Interview —
  Elizabeth Gilbert
The Moth Podcast —
  The Alpha Wolf: Elizabeth
  Gilbert

Radio
BBC Radio 4: *We Need to Talk
  about Death*, series 1–3

Watch

Films
About Time
Groundhog Day

Documentaries
End Game (Netflix)
Beyond Goodbye
One More Time with Feeling
  — Nick Cave
*Dying Is Not as Bad as You
  Think* — BBC.com ideas

Online

doingdeath.com
deathcafe.com
theartofdying.net (Vol 1,2,3)
thoughtsinpassing.com
orderofthegooddeath.com
monbiot.com
  search *'The Gift of Death'*

Talks

The Do Lectures
Alastair Humphreys
Giles Duley
Katie Elliott
Kris Hallenga

TED Talks
The Power of Vulnerability
  by Brene Brown
*What Really Matters in
  the End?'*
  by B.J. Miller
*There's More to Life Than
  Being Happy*
  by Emily Esfahani Smith
What Makes a Good Life?
  by Robert Waldinger

About the Author

Amanda Blainey is a speaker and activist in the growing death movement. After twenty years working as a creative producer and agent in the advertising industry, she wanted to follow a more meaningful path. She founded Doing Death, a multi-media platform and podcast that opens up authentic conversations about death and dying to inspire people to live more fully. In addition to volunteering at a local hospice in the UK, she is involved in a charity that records the life stories of terminally ill patients. Currently Amanda is training to be a death doula and regularly runs a local Death Café. She spoke at the Do Lectures in 2018.

@doingdeath
doingdeath.com

Thanks

To Michael Blainey, you are my light, my love, my inspiration. Thank you for your patience, your kindness, your encouragement, your never-ending belief in me. And for doing something you love, I'm so proud of you. If your love for me is as good as it gets then I'll die a happy woman.

To my children Pearl, Rose and Ruben, you are my biggest teachers.

To my mum, Carmen Scanes, for her candid parenting and teaching me that death is a normal part of life.

To my sister Melissa Hastie for being alongside me in our crazy mad life. We truly are the 'sisters of death'.

To Dave Hieatt for using his gut instinct (as usual) and taking a punt on me.

To Emily Mathieson *@aerendeshop* for your business acumen and advice. For your quest for a more sustainable life. For being a stickler for grammar and use of Aerende props in the Resources photograph.

To Sam Rudd for letting me share your story and for being one of the most sparkling, courageous and brave women I know.

To all my close friends, Emma Cooper, Mandy Bonner, Cara Humphreys, Faith Robertson, Marie Mitchell, Ella Poyner, Bobby Sebire, Cam Mitchell, Dan Moorey and Rach Thorlby, for inspiring me, supporting me, loving me, making me laugh and being lifelong friends throughout the years.

To Ian Hands for all your incredible typography, design and help you have given me over the years in all my ventures. You are unique in everything you do.

To Josie Raison for listening and for giving me your yoga space to inspire and move me.

To Derek Seagrim for planning a beautiful funeral for your gorgeous and much-missed wife Antoinette. And for showing me how to live with vigour in your seventies!

To Sarah Johnson for your intuition, friendship, coffee meetings and guidance on this book.

To Lorna Caddy for her legal advice. My neighbourhood just keeps on giving!

To Sarah Brown for giving me pep talks and encouragement in the school pick-up queue (sometimes all you need are those little chats).

To Barbara Altounyan for giving me the opportunity to record people's life stories for *@hospicebiog*.

To Ed Bevin at the *fleetvillelarder.com* for the space to let people talk about death and for taking the risk with your own venture (not to mention the best cheese!)

To Carlo Constandinou for being a great teacher and listener (and my cranial osteopath).

To Miranda West, my editor and publisher, for giving me this platform and her faith in me.

To Anna Hunt, 'The Shaman in Stilettos', who helped me heal from past wounds and release the stuff that no longer served me.

To Allistair Anderson at Compassionate Funerals for his advice.

To Josefine Speyer for being a goddess death educator; the world needs more people like you.

To Michele Knight for inspiring me every day on Instagram with your words. You are a warrior woman.

To Jo Marovitch and her team and the incredible work you do.

To Sue Parkhill *@parkhillphoto* for your beautiful photography and journeying with me on my madcap adventures.

To Janet Blainey for some down-under pointers.

To Nicola Bensley for finding a person's true spirit in your photographs.

To Penny Verity, the most glamorous lady. Thank you for sharing your most wonderful planning tips for death preparation. And thanks to Maggie Telfer for introducing us.

Finally, to all the people who have taught me about death and shown me how to live.

Index

Notes

Books in the series

Do Beekeeping
Orren Fox

Do Birth
Caroline Flint

Do Breathe
Michael Townsend
Williams

Do Death
Amanda Blainey

Do Design
Alan Moore

Do Disrupt
Mark Shayler

Do Fly
Gavin Strange

Do Grow
Alice Holden

Do Improvise
Robert Poynton

Do Inhabit
Sue Fan, Danielle
Quigley

Do Lead
Les McKeown

Do Listen
Bobette Buster

Do Open
David Hieatt

Do Pause
Robert Poynton

Do Preserve
Anja Dunk, Jen Goss,
Mimi Beaven

Do Protect
Johnathan Rees

Do Purpose
David Hieatt

Do Scale
Les McKeown

Do Sea Salt
Alison, David & Jess
Lea-Wilson

Do Sing
James Sills

Do Sourdough
Andrew Whitley

Do Story
Bobette Buster

Do Wild Baking
Tom Herbert

Also available

Path
A short story about reciprocity
Louisa Thomsen Brits

The Skimming Stone
A short story about courage
Dominic Wilcox

Stay Curious
How we created a world class
event in a cowshed
Clare Hieatt

Available in print and
digital formats from
bookshops, online
retailers or via our
website: **thedobook.co**

To hear about events and
forthcoming titles, you can
find us on social media
@dobookco, or subscribe
to our newsletter